LIVING WITH
ASTHMA

Peta Bee

HODDER
Wayland

an imprint of Hodder Children's Books

Titles in the series
Living with Asthma
Living with Blindness
Living with Cerebral Palsy
Living with Deafness
Living with Diabetes
Living with Down's Syndrome
Living with Epilepsy
Living with Leukaemia

Series and book editor: Cath Senker
Cover design: Steve Wheele Design
Book design: Peter Laws
Consultant: Nick Tapp, Acting Chief Executive, East Sussex Disability Association

First published in 1998 by Wayland Publishers Ltd

This edition published in 2000 by Hodder Wayland, an imprint of Hodder Children's Books

British Library Cataloguing in Publication Data
Bee, Peta
  Living with Asthma
  1. Asthma – Juvenile literature
  I. Title II. Asthma
  616.2'38

ISBN 0 7502 2837 7

Printed and bound by G. Canale and C.S.p.A., Italy

Picture acknowledgements
Hodder Wayland would like to thank: Ace cover (top), (Auschrombs) 28; Eye Ubiquitous (Paul Thompson) 7, (David Cumming) 24; Getty Images (Andrew Syred) 8; Robert Harding cover (middle), (Dr Muller) 20; James Davies Travel Photography 16; National Asthma Campaign 29; Skjold 19; Wayland (Jeff Greenberg) 14, (Howard Davies) 15 (below).
All the other photographs were taken for Hodder Wayland by Angela Hampton.
Most of the people who are photographed in this book are models.
The illustration on page 6 is by Michael Courtney.

While every effort has been made to secure permission, in one case it has proved impossible to trace the copyright holder.

Hodder Children's Books, a division of Hodder Headline Plc,
338 Euston Road, London, NW1 3BH

Contents

Meet Rachel, John and Nicola

Rachel, John and Nicola are children like you. They are about your age and go to schools like yours. After school and at the weekends they are all very busy doing things that they enjoy.

Rachel is a keen swimmer. She belongs to a swimming club and swims in her local pool twice a week. Her favourite stroke is backstroke and she hopes that, one day, she will win a gold medal swimming in the Olympic Games.

△ Rachel works hard at her swimming. She is one of the fastest swimmers in her school.

John prefers to play football and take part in athletics. He is in the school football team and practises his football skills every day when he gets home. He is also a very fast runner and finished first in a race at his school sports day this summer.

◁ John's ambition is to play football for his country.

▽ Nicola and her friends spend hours practising dance routines.

Nicola loves being with her best friends. They enjoy listening to music and dancing.

Rachel, John and Nicola all lead very different lives. But they have one thing in common. Each of them has a condition called asthma. Millions of people in Britain have asthma, so they are not alone. Asthma is serious because it can make breathing difficult, but it doesn't mean you have to stop enjoying yourself. Rachel, John and Nicola have all learned to take control of their asthma so that they can enjoy all their favourite activities.

What is asthma?

Asthma is a condition that affects the airways – the small tubes that carry air in and out of the lungs. People with asthma may feel short of breath so that they wheeze or cough. Sometimes it can leave their chest feeling tight and uncomfortable.

When people have asthma, their airways are sensitive. If they come into contact with something called an asthma trigger, their airways may become inflamed. This can happen if they catch a cold or if they breathe in other allergens (things that they are allergic to).

An asthma trigger is something that makes asthma worse. Some of the most common asthma triggers are colds, or other virus infections.

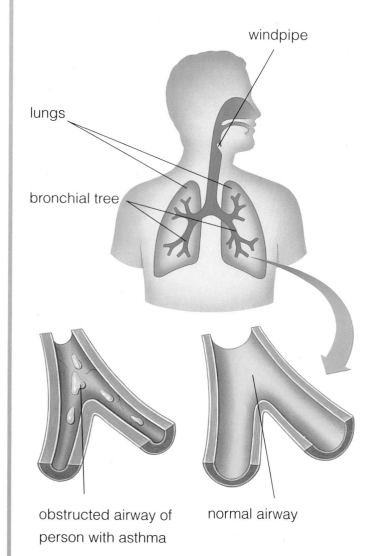

windpipe

lungs

bronchial tree

obstructed airway of
person with asthma

normal airway

◁ This diagram shows
how the airways are
affected by asthma.

△ Traffic fumes make some people's asthma worse.

John's asthma is made worse by house-dust mites and cat fur. His grandmother has a cat called Jessie, so John has to be careful when he visits. Nicola's asthma is triggered by traffic fumes and poor air quality. Grass pollen, poor air quality and exercise make Rachel's asthma worse.

If people who have asthma come into contact with their asthma triggers, they find it hard to breathe. It can be quite frightening when this happens. But special asthma medicine can help them to breathe normally.

If you have asthma, it is important to know which things trigger your asthma so that you can try to avoid them.

What is a house-dust mite?

House-dust mites are triggers for many people with asthma. They are very small (about 0.3 mm long), so you can't see them without a microscope. But there could be as many as 2 million of them living in your mattress!

The mites live in dust that builds up around the house. They live just about everywhere – in carpets, curtains, bedclothes and soft furniture, such as sofas and armchairs.

△ A house-dust mite, about 1,000 times bigger than its real size.

The main problem for people with asthma is the droppings left behind by house-dust mites. Although the droppings are tiny, they float in the air with dust so that it is easy to breathe them in. If people with asthma breathe in the droppings, they can irritate their airways and trigger asthma.

There are lots of things you can do to reduce the number of house-dust mites in your home. Make sure your room is dusted regularly with a damp cloth and keep all your clothes in the wardrobe. Piles of clothes on the floor make the perfect home for house-dust mites. Open the bedroom window in the morning too. House-dust mites don't like cold air.

◁ Dusting with a damp cloth regularly helps to keep down the dust in the bedroom.

How asthma medicine can help

There are lots of medicines that make it easier for people with asthma to live normal lives. Before giving out medicine, the doctor may measure your breathing with something called a peak flow meter and will ask about your symptoms. Then she (or the nurse) will give you some asthma medicine to breathe in, usually using devices called inhalers.

Rachel's doctor gave her two special inhalers that help her to breathe more easily. One is called a reliever and the other is called a preventer. Both medicines contain drugs that help to control her asthma.

△ The doctor is showing Rachel the reliever inhaler.

▷ Rachel is learning how to use her preventer inhaler.

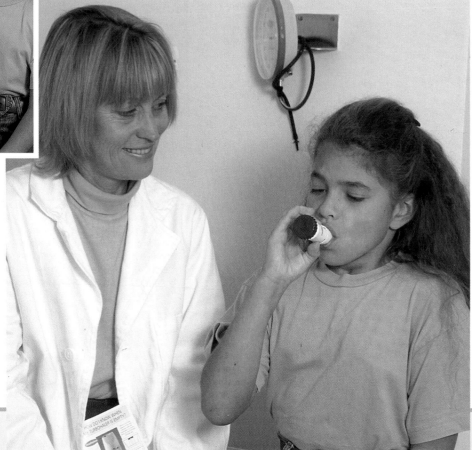

▷ Rachel uses her reliever inhaler when she feels her breathing is becoming worse.

Rachel's reliever inhaler

'My reliever inhaler is blue. I use it when I first feel my asthma coming on. It makes the muscles in my airways relax so I can breathe easily again. I can't always tell when I might get asthma symptoms, so I always carry my reliever inhaler with me.'

Rachel has a brown preventer inhaler that helps calm down her airways. She uses it first thing in the morning and last thing at night, even when she is well. Not all preventer inhalers are brown; some are white, orange or red. Many preventer inhalers contain a low dose of steroids. Using a preventer inhaler means that Rachel is less likely to have an asthma attack if she comes into contact with her asthma triggers. This is one way for her to keep her asthma under control.

Avoiding asthma triggers at home

If people with asthma come into contact with their triggers all the time, they are likely to have asthma symptoms more often. John's mother, Gina, is careful to help John avoid his asthma triggers around their home. There are lots of things she can do to protect him.

John has special covers for his mattress, duvet and pillow. These are made from a material that keeps the dust mites inside, so that he can't breathe in the droppings when he is asleep. Gina washes John's bedclothes at a hot temperature every week to get rid of mite droppings. She also vacuums his bedroom often.

∇ It is a good idea to vacuum every day, using a good vacuum cleaner that does not spread the dust around.

Gina opens the windows every day to let in plenty of fresh air. House-dust mites don't like cold, fresh air! She also dusts the furniture with a damp cloth to remove any mites. Instead of curtains, which gather dust, their house has window blinds.

▷ Gina makes sure the kitchen window is open when John helps her to cook, to reduce condensation.

House-dust mites love warm, damp air. A de-humidifier device may help to reduce the dampness in the air that can encourage house-dust mites to live in your home. Gina always keeps the kitchen door closed when she is cooking to stop the dampness from spreading to other parts of the house.

When Rachel plays outside, she tries to avoid things that will make her asthma worse. Grass pollen is the main problem, but the pollen in flowers can also trigger her asthma. Rachel does not bring fresh flowers into the house.

◁ Rachel is allergic to grass pollen, but she can play outside if she is careful.

Exercise is good for you

Exercise is a great way to keep fit and have fun. Unfortunately, it is also one of the most common asthma triggers. Everyone gets out of breath when they exercise, but if you have exercise asthma you will wheeze and cough after the exercise has stopped. If this happens to you, you should tell your doctor or asthma nurse the next time you visit.

◁ Keeping fit is just as important for people with asthma as for anyone else.

Having asthma doesn't mean you should stop exercising. In fact, regular exercise can actually help your asthma. The fitter you get, the better your lungs work and the fewer problems you should have with asthma.

Some sports are less likely to bring on asthma than others. Cricket, tennis and sprinting, where the exercise is in short bursts, tend not to trigger asthma.

▷ The warm, damp air in the pool helps to relieve Rachel's airways.

Swimming is a good choice for some people whose asthma is helped by damp air. The air at pools is damp and warm so it doesn't irritate their lungs.

Exercise is a trigger for Rachel's asthma, but she has learnt to make sure that her swimming doesn't cause her to have an asthma attack.

Rachel uses her preventer inhaler every day. Before she exercises, she takes her reliever inhaler. Then she warms up by doing some short sprints in the hallway before she goes into the swimming pool. This means that doing exercise isn't such a shock to her system.

◁ Having asthma doesn't mean you can't become successful at sport.

What about pets?

Pets can be great fun. John loves animals, especially cats, and would love to have a kitten of his own. But animals are a common trigger for asthma. When John comes into contact with pet fur or bird feathers, it makes his asthma worse.

If you have asthma, it is a good idea not to keep pets that have feathers or fur. But it is not only animal hair that can cause problems. Tiny flakes of animal skin can get into the air with dust and be breathed in by people with asthma. Even the urine of pets such as cats, dogs, guinea pigs, rabbits and gerbils can cause problems for some people.

There are just a few pets such as stick insects and goldfish that may not cause problems. But that doesn't mean that people with asthma have to stay away from animals altogether.

▷ It is important to brush pets regularly to remove loose fur.

▷ If you have asthma, it is not a good idea to keep a cat as a pet. Even when the cat goes outside, the cat allergens can stay in the house for several hours.

The saliva left on a cat's fur after it has washed can also trigger asthma. To make sure John is protected, his grandmother always wipes her cat's fur with a damp cloth before John visits. This gets rid of the saliva. She also keeps Jessie out of the living room and kitchen whenever she can. John always makes sure that he washes his hands after stroking the cat's fur.

Going on holiday

When John goes on holiday with his family, he makes plans well in advance to make sure he enjoys it as much as everyone else.

▽ John collects together all of his asthma medicines to make sure he does not forget anything.

Being away from home means lots of changes and there are many things that can trigger asthma on holiday. There is no one holiday destination that is the best place to go for people with asthma, because everyone's asthma is so different.

John is prepared

'Before I leave, I make sure I've packed enough of my asthma medicine to last the whole holiday. I pack spare inhalers just in case I lose one. Also, I carry on taking my preventer medicine before we actually go, and while we're on holiday. That means I'm less likely to have problems while we're away.'

◁ Choosing a cool place to go on holiday may help some people with asthma.

Weather conditions, pollen levels and air pollution will vary wherever you go. Some people with asthma find that certain weather conditions make their asthma worse. If John and his family go abroad, they choose a place where the weather is warm, but not very hot. Dry, hot places can be dusty. The dust might irritate John's airways. John's older brother, Steven, keeps an eye on the local weather changes when they are on holiday.

Poor air quality

Unfortunately, the air we breathe is not always clean and fresh. The quality of air is often poor and contains lots of different things that can make asthma worse. Outdoor air contains natural triggers such as pollen and ground-level ozone.

◁ It is hard to avoid traffic fumes. Breathing in outdoor air can trigger your asthma.

Air also contains unnatural pollutants. Car exhaust fumes release gases and small particles into the air. There are other pollutants, such as cigarette smoke. Sometimes the levels of these pollutants can irritate the lungs of people with asthma.

Nicola protects herself

'When it's really cold, I wrap a
scarf over my nose and mouth
when I'm walking to school.
It keeps out the cold air. I find I
wheeze and cough less then.'

△ Breathing through
a scarf can warm
the air you take into
your lungs.

Every day Nicola's family listens to a forecast for air
pollution levels. The forecast will say if there will be high
levels of certain gases, such as nitrogen dioxide and ozone, in
the air that day.

If poor air quality triggers your asthma, it is better not to do
too much exercise outdoors on very hot summer afternoons,
when ground-level ozone levels are at their highest.

What to do in an emergency

Emma is Rachel's best friend. She doesn't have asthma but she knows what to do if Rachel has an asthma attack when she is around. Emma and Rachel know that asthma can be very dangerous, so they both make sure they are well prepared in case of emergency.

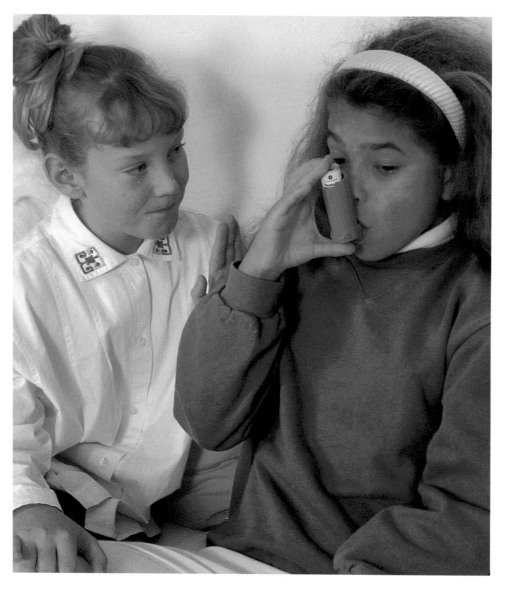

◁ Rachel has learnt exactly what to do in an emergency, and how to use her inhaler correctly. Emma has also learnt all about Rachel's different medicines.

▷ Emma's dad has called for anambulance. Now Emma is calling Rachel's mum to tell her that Rachel is not well.

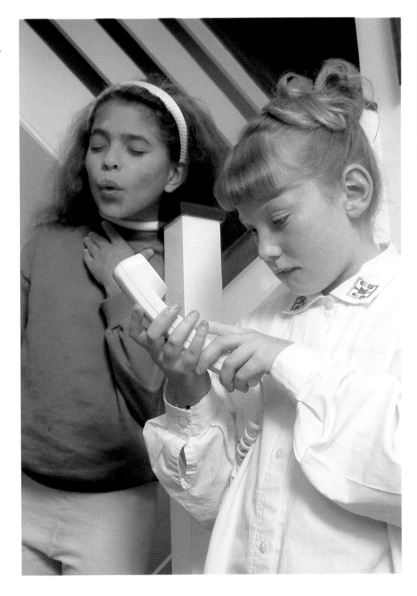

First Emma tries to keep Rachel calm by talking to her. Although this is not easy when Rachel is finding it hard to breathe, Emma knows that panicking will only make things worse. Then she gets Rachel to sit up straight and tells her to breathe slowly and calmly.

Emma knows that Rachel always keeps her reliever inhaler in her school bag, so she fetches it and Rachel takes two puffs straight away. If Rachel is still not feeling better after a few minutes, Emma will go and fetch an adult, who may need to call for an ambulance. Rachel will keep taking her inhaler every five to ten minutes until medical help arrives.

If Emma isn't around when she has an asthma attack, Rachel knows that she needs to tell an adult to get medical help quickly, especially if she thinks her inhaler isn't working properly.

How would you manage?

Have you ever wondered what it's like to have asthma? Remember, like Rachel, Nicola and John, if you have asthma, you have it all the time. Your airways are always sensitive, although you only have asthma symptoms when you come into contact with one of your triggers, or forget to take your medicine.

Asthma will be present all day every day and it can affect everything you do. We have seen that there are lots of things that can be done to help people with asthma to lead normal lives.

△ Everyone needs exercise to keep fit. If they take care, people with asthma can enjoy sport like everybody else.

▷ People with asthma are no different to anyone else, but sometimes they have to make changes to their lives.

Think about the sort of problems that people with asthma might face every day. Write down what you would do to reduce these problems if you had asthma.

Think about the different things that trigger asthma away from home. What kind of things could you do to lessen asthma triggers in cold weather? What would you do before you took part in sport?

Write down what you would do to avoid three different asthma triggers such as poor air quality, house-dust mites and pollen.

Making life easier

△ John's spacer device helps his asthma medicine to work quickly.

Life can be made easier in many ways for people with asthma. Children like John, Nicola and Rachel take different kinds of medicine to help them to control their asthma.

Not all asthma medicines are suitable for everyone, so doctors and nurses help people with asthma decide which ones are best for them. There are tablets and a variety of inhalers that contain mild steroids. These are medicines that help to make the airways less swollen. Taken regularly, these medicines will help to control asthma.

There are other ways to make life easier too. John uses a spacer device to take his preventer treatment every morning and evening. This can help the medicine to reach his airways, where it is needed most.

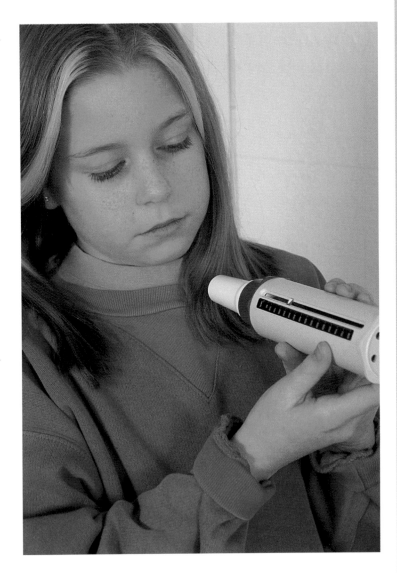

▽ A peak flow meter shows Nicola how well she is breathing.

Nicola checks her peak flow regularly to keep track of how good or bad her asthma is at any time. Peak flow meters measure how hard you can blow out. When Nicola's asthma is under control, she can blow out a lot of air and her peak flow reading is higher. Nicola also monitors her asthma symptoms.

Sometimes Rachel's asthma is really bad and she finds it hard to control her symptoms. Then, Rachel's doctor prescribes some steroid tablets for her. These contain a higher dose of medicine and she takes them for just a few days until her asthma is back under control.

Rachel, John and Nicola have all learnt to take important steps to control their asthma.

Getting help

There are many places where you can get advice, information and support about living with asthma.

Your doctor and asthma nurse will be able to give you advice on the type of asthma medicine that is best for you. They are there to help you. Always talk to them if you are worried about anything linked to asthma.

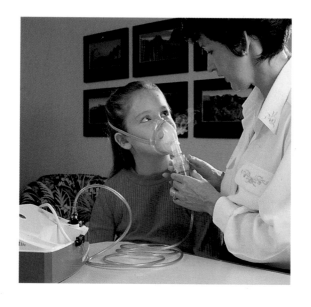

The National Asthma Campaign is a charity that helps to keep the millions of people with asthma in touch with the latest developments in asthma research. It also produces a range of booklets giving advice and information about everything from exercise and asthma to asthma and holidays. It is the biggest asthma charity in the UK. There is a special club for young people with asthma and a magazine called *A for Asthma*. You can get an application form to join the Junior Asthma Club from the National Asthma Campaign's headquarters.

△ Talking to an asthma nurse will provide answers to the questions you may have about your asthma.

You can contact the National Asthma Campaign at Providence House, Providence Place, London N1 0NT, tel. (0207) 226 2260 or, if you live in Scotland, contact National Asthma Campaign Scotland, 21 Coates Crescent, Edinburgh EH3 7AF, tel. (0131) 226 2544.

If you have problems with asthma, the National Asthma Campaign has an Asthma Helpline that you can call to speak to a special asthma nurse. Call the Asthma Helpline on 0345 010203, Monday to Friday between 9 am and 7 pm.

If you have a computer linked to the internet, you can contact the National Asthma Campaign website. It is at http://www.asthma.org.uk.

▷ Young people on a holiday arranged by the National Asthma Campaign.

There are also regional National Asthma Campaign groups where people meet to discuss issues surrounding asthma. You and your parents or carers are welcome to go along to the local meetings in your area. Contact the Campaign's headquarters for details of your nearest branch.

Local newspapers and radio stations provide air quality forecasts. You can also call the Department of the Environment's Pollution Helpline on 0800 556677 (calls are free). This is a recorded message with a general comment about pollution levels. Similar information is available on Teletext (page 106) and Ceefax (page 404).

Glossary

Allergen Anything that causes an allergic reaction, often particular foods, pollen, fur or dust.

Asthma trigger Something that causes asthma symptoms to become worse.

Condensation When water vapour turns to water, often on a window.

Ground-level ozone Bright sunlight makes a chemical reaction in the air, which produces ozone at ground level. This ground-level ozone can inflame the airways of people with asthma.

Inflammation When a part of the body is inflamed, it becomes hot, red and sore.

Inhaler A device for breathing medicine into the lungs, through the mouth.

Peak flow The measurement of how much air you can blow out.

Pollutants Substances that damage the environment. Small particles of pollutants in the air can make breathing difficult and trigger asthma in some people.

Preventer inhaler A device that contains drugs which calm down the airways so that an asthma attack is less likely to happen.

Reliever inhaler A device that contains drugs which relax the muscles in the airways so that it is easier to breathe.

Spacer device A device that is used with an inhaler to help a person to breathe in more medication.

Steroids Drugs that make the airways less swollen.

Symptom A change in a person's health that can show that he or she has a disease. A symptom is something you feel or see, like a pain or rash.

Further information

Asthma at your Fingertips (revised edition) by Mark Levy et. al. (Class Publishing, 1994)

The Asthma Handbook by Jenny Lewis (Vermilion, an imprint of Ebury Press, 1995)

Asthma and Wendy Wheeze by Julie Alfrey (Children's Meducational Books, 1994)

Conquering Asthma (revised edition) by Peter Barnes and Michael Newhouse (Manson Publishing, 1994)

Jane has Asthma by Nigel Snell (Hamish Hamilton, 1991)

Living with Asthma and Hay Fever (revised edition) by John Donaldson (Penguin Health, 1994)

Thomas has Asthma by Andrew Pattison (Hyland House Publishing, Australia, 1988)

AUDIO CASSETTE

Coping with Asthma available from Asthma Tape,
PO Box 1, Wirral L47 7DD
A 30-minute tape covering the basic details about asthma.

VIDEOS

Aiming High by Action Asthma, available from Aiming High Video Offer, Dept BD 2426, Freepost, Bradford, West Yorkshire BD7 2YD

Away with the Wheeze available from Dave Knowles Films,
34 Ashleigh Close, Butts Ash Hythe, Hampshire SO45 3QP
A video for parents about childhood asthma.

Desmond Dragon TV by Action Asthma. Available from Desmond Dragon Video Offer, Dept BD 2426, Freepost, Bradford, West Yorkshire BD7 2YD
A video aimed at children aged 4 to 11.

Further leaflets, videos and tapes can be obtained from the National Asthma Campaign at the address mentioned on pages 28–9.
The British Allergy Foundation, Deepdene House, 30 Bellegrove Road, Welling Kent DA16 3BV publishes a range of leaflets and information about asthma and related conditions.

Index

Numbers in **bold** show subjects shown in pictures.